HEALING

THE NARCISSISTIC

WOUND

Recovery and Transformation For Men, Women and Kids

AULYN BILL

CONTENTS

INTRODUCTION   4

CHAPTER 1: UNDERSTANDING NARCISSISM   8

   Narcissism and its forms   8

   The origins in nature vs. nurture   14

   DSM-5 criteria   17

   Common traits and behaviors   19

CHAPTER 2: THE GREAT CONSEQUENCES   23

   Effects on relationships   23

   Performance and career success   26

   Physical and mental health   29

   Legal and financial potential   32

   Impact of social media   35

CHAPTER 3: THE ROAD TO RECOVERY   38

   Recognizing and acknowledging tendencies   38

   Steps to change behavior patterns   41

   Real-life individuals success   44

Role of therapy and support recovery 46

CHAPTER 4: STRATEGIES FOR MEN 49

Recognizing tendencies in men 49

Specific strategies for men 52

Tips for navigating work and career 55

CHAPTER 5: STRATEGIES FOR WOMEN 59

Recognizing tendencies in women 59

Specific strategies for women to overcome 61

Tips for balancing career and family 64

CHAPTER 6: STRATEGIES FOR KIDS AND TEENS 68

Signs in children and teenagers 68

Tips for healthy self-esteem 70

Parent Strategic modeling and prevention 73

CONCLUSION 76

INTRODUCTION

Narcissism is a personality trait characterized by excessive self-love, self-admiration, and self-centeredness. People with narcissistic tendencies have an inflated sense of their own importance and are often preoccupied with fantasies of unlimited success, power, beauty, or intelligence.

They may demand constant attention and admiration, and have a strong need for control and admiration from others. While some degree of self-confidence and self-love is healthy, excessive narcissism can have harmful effects on both the individual and those around them.

Narcissistic individuals often have difficulty empathizing with others, which can lead to a lack of consideration for others' feelings, needs, and rights. They may exploit others for their own gain, manipulate them to maintain control, or become abusive when their needs are not met.

One of the most harmful effects of narcissism is its impact on relationships. Narcissistic individuals may struggle to form deep and meaningful connections with others, as their preoccupation with themselves often overshadows their interest in and empathy for others.

This can lead to a cycle of failed relationships, as others become exhausted by the narcissist's self-centeredness and inability to relate to others.

Furthermore, narcissism can also have negative consequences on the individual's mental and physical health. Narcissistic individuals may become anxious or depressed when their inflated sense of self is threatened or not met, leading to a fragile sense of self-worth.

They may also struggle with substance abuse or other destructive behaviors as a means of coping with their emotional distress. In addition to the negative effects on personal relationships and mental health, narcissistic behavior can also have legal and financial consequences.

Narcissistic individuals may engage in unethical or illegal behaviors to maintain their sense of control or satisfy their desires for power or recognition. This can lead to criminal charges, lawsuits, or other legal consequences, as well as significant financial losses.

Estimates on the prevalence of narcissism vary depending on the definition and assessment methods used. However, research suggests that narcissistic traits are relatively common in society.

It is worth noting that narcissism is not limited to one gender, age group, or cultural background. While some studies suggest that men are more likely to exhibit narcissistic traits than women, others have found narcissism may be more common in younger generations, other studies have found no significant age-related differences.

Overall, it can have negative effects on both the individual and those around them.

The book "How to Stop Being a Narcissist: Real and Proven Strategies for Men, Women, and Kids" is a comprehensive guide to understanding and overcoming narcissism.

The purpose of the book is to provide readers with real and proven strategies for recognizing and addressing their own narcissistic tendencies, and to help them build healthier relationships with others.

The book is organized into six chapters, beginning with an introduction to narcissism and its harmful effects on oneself and others. The book aims to help readers recognize and overcome narcissism, and to build deeper and more meaningful relationships with others.

By providing real and proven strategies for addressing narcissistic tendencies, the book empowers readers to take control of their own behavior and lead healthier, more fulfilling lives.

CHAPTER 1

UNDERSTANDING NARCISSISM

Narcissism and its forms

Narcissism is a personality trait characterized by an excessive focus on oneself, a grandiose sense of self-importance, a need for admiration, and a lack of empathy for others. It is a pattern of behavior that is rooted in deep-seated insecurities and feelings of inadequacy, and can take several different forms.

Grandiose narcissism

Grandiose narcissism is one of the subtypes of narcissistic personality disorder (NPD). Individuals with grandiose narcissism have an inflated sense of self-importance and believe that they are special or unique. They often have a sense of entitlement, expecting others to meet their needs without reciprocation. They may also lack empathy and have a tendency to exploit others for their own benefit.

Some common characteristics of grandiose narcissism include:

Exaggerated sense of self-importance: Individuals with grandiose narcissism often believe that they are better than others and deserve special treatment.

Fantasies of power and success: They may have grandiose fantasies of wealth, power, and success, and may engage in self-promotion to achieve these goals.

Need for admiration: They crave attention and admiration from others, and may become angry or defensive when they feel their status is threatened.

Lack of empathy: They may have difficulty recognizing or caring about the feelings of others, and may use others for their own benefit without guilt or remorse.

Entitlement: They may believe that they are entitled to special treatment or privileges, and may become angry or aggressive when they don't get what they want.

It is important to note that not all individuals with grandiose tendencies have NPD, and not all individuals with NPD exhibit grandiose tendencies. However, grandiose narcissism is one of the most commonly recognized subtypes of NPD and can have significant negative impacts on both the individual and those around them.

Vulnerable narcissism

Vulnerable narcissism is another subtype of narcissistic personality disorder (NPD). Individuals with vulnerable narcissism often have low self-esteem and may feel insecure or inferior to others. They may use their narcissism as a defense mechanism to protect themselves from feelings of shame, rejection, or failure.

Some common characteristics of vulnerable narcissism include:

Hypersensitivity: Individuals with vulnerable narcissism may be highly sensitive to criticism or rejection, and may respond with anger, defensiveness, or withdrawal.

Insecurity: They may feel insecure or inferior to others, and may seek validation or reassurance from others to feel better about themselves.

Covert behavior: They may engage in more covert or subtle forms of self-promotion, such as bragging or fishing for compliments.

Emotional instability: They may experience intense emotions, such as anxiety, depression, or mood swings, and may struggle with self-regulation.

Victim mentality: They may adopt a victim mentality, believing that others are out to get them or that they are unfairly treated or misunderstood.

It is important to note that vulnerable narcissism can be just as damaging as grandiose narcissism, if not more so. Individuals with vulnerable narcissism may be more prone to self-destructive behaviors, such as substance abuse or self-harm, and may struggle with interpersonal relationships.

Malignant narcissism

A subtype of narcissistic personality disorder (NPD) that is portrayed by a combination of narcissistic and antisocial traits is Malignant narcissism. Individuals with malignant narcissism often display a pervasive pattern of grandiosity, a lack of empathy for others, and a willingness to exploit or manipulate others to achieve their own goals.

Some common characteristics of malignant narcissism include:

Aggression: Individuals with malignant narcissism may be prone to anger, hostility, and aggression, and may lash out at others who challenge their sense of superiority.

Manipulation: They may use manipulation tactics, such as gaslighting or triangulation, to control or deceive others and maintain their sense of power.

Lack of empathy: They may have difficulty empathizing with others and may disregard or exploit the needs and feelings of those around them.

Entitlement: They may have a strong sense of entitlement and may believe that they are entitled to special treatment or privileges, regardless of the impact on others.

Paranoia: They may be prone to paranoia or conspiracy thinking and may believe that others are out to get them or that they are unfairly targeted or persecuted.

It is important to note that individuals with malignant narcissism may be at an increased risk for engaging in harmful or criminal behavior, such as domestic violence, sexual assault, or fraud. Treatment for malignant narcissism can be challenging, but therapy and other interventions may be helpful in addressing underlying psychological and behavioral issues and reducing the risk of harm to others.

It is worth noting that while these three forms of narcissism are often discussed separately, they can also coexist and overlap in individuals. For example, a person with grandiose narcissism may also exhibit vulnerable traits when their sense of superiority is threatened, while a person with vulnerable narcissism may engage in manipulative or exploitative behavior to maintain their fragile sense of self-esteem.

The origins in nature vs. nurture

The origins of narcissism are complex and multifaceted, and can be influenced by a combination of genetic, environmental, and social factors. The nature vs. nurture debate has long been a topic of discussion when it comes to understanding the development of narcissistic traits.

On the nature side

Research has suggested that genetic factors may play a role in the development of narcissism. Twin studies have found that narcissistic traits have a moderate to high degree of heritability, meaning that a significant proportion of individual differences in narcissism can be attributed to genetic factors. For example, a study of adolescent twins found that genetic factors accounted for approximately 40 percent of the variance in narcissism scores, while environmental factors accounted for the remaining 60 percent.

On the nurture side

Environmental factors such as parenting styles, childhood experiences, and social and cultural influences can also contribute to the development of narcissistic traits. For example, a study found that children who experienced parental overvaluation, or excessive praise and admiration, were more likely to develop narcissistic traits. Similarly, exposure to societal messages that prioritize individual achievement and success over collective values may also contribute to the development of narcissistic traits.

It is worth noting that the interplay between nature and nurture is complex, and that genetic and environmental factors may interact with one another in complex ways to shape the development of narcissism. For example, a study found that individuals with a genetic predisposition towards impulsivity and sensation-seeking were more likely to develop narcissistic traits if they also experienced childhood maltreatment.

while the origins of narcissism are complex and multifaceted, research suggests that both genetic and environmental factors can contribute to the development of narcissistic traits.

Understanding the interplay between these factors can be helpful in developing strategies for preventing and addressing narcissistic tendencies, and in building healthier relationships with others.

DSM-5 criteria

A mental health condition represented by a pervasive pattern of grandiosity, a need for admiration, and a lack of empathy is Narcissistic Personality Disorder (NPD). The Diagnostic and Statistical Manual of Mental Disorders, Fifth Edition (DSM-5) outlines the following criteria for the diagnosis of NPD:

Grandiosity: An inflated sense of self-importance and superiority. Individuals with grandiosity may believe that they are special, unique, or better than others, and may have an exaggerated sense of their abilities, achievements, or talents.

Some common signs of grandiosity include:
Exaggerated self-importance, Entitlement, Arrogance, Fantasies of power or success and Disregard for others

It is important to note that grandiosity can be harmful to relationships, treatment often involves addressing underlying psychological and emotional issues, such as low self-esteem, and developing healthier coping mechanisms and communication skills.

Need for admiration: A need for excessive admiration.

Lack of empathy: A lack of empathy, as indicated by a lack of concern for the feelings of others or a tendency to exploit or take advantage of others.

Beginning in early adulthood: The symptoms of NPD must begin in early adulthood and be stable over time.

Impairment in functioning: The grandiosity, need for admiration, and lack of empathy must cause significant impairment in functioning, such as impairments in social, occupational, or other important areas of life.

Not due to another disorder: The symptoms of NPD cannot be better explained by another mental disorder, such as bipolar disorder or borderline personality disorder.

Distinguishing features: Additional distinguishing features of NPD may include a sense of entitlement, a preoccupation with fantasies of unlimited success, power, brilliance, or beauty, a belief that one is special or unique, and a tendency to exploit others for personal gain.

It is important to note that not all individuals with narcissistic traits meet the criteria for a diagnosis of NPD. Furthermore, a diagnosis of NPD should only be made by a qualified psychiatrist after a comprehensive evaluation of a person's symptoms and medical history.

Common traits and behaviors

Narcissism is a personality trait characterized by a sense of grandiosity, self-importance, and a lack of empathy towards others. While not all individuals with narcissistic traits meet the criteria for a diagnosis of Narcissistic Personality Disorder (NPD), there are several common traits and behaviors associated with narcissism, including:

Grandiosity: Narcissistic individuals tend to have an inflated sense of self-importance and a belief that they are superior to others.

Need for admiration: Narcissistic individuals have a constant need for attention and admiration from others, and may seek out praise and recognition.

Lack of empathy: Narcissistic individuals have a limited ability to understand and relate to the feelings of others, and may be dismissive or insensitive to the needs of others.

Sense of entitlement: Narcissistic individuals may believe that they are entitled to special treatment, privileges, or recognition due to their perceived superiority.

Manipulative behavior: Narcissistic individuals may use manipulation or coercion to get what they want from others, and may be prone to lying, cheating, or exploiting others.

Fragile self-esteem: Despite their grandiosity, narcissistic individuals may have fragile self-esteem that is easily threatened by criticism or perceived rejection.

Difficulty with relationships: Narcissistic individuals may struggle to maintain healthy relationships with others, as their self-centered behavior and lack of empathy can lead to conflict and resentment.

Envy and jealousy: Narcissistic individuals may feel threatened by the success or achievements of others, and may experience envy or jealousy.

Lack of accountability: Narcissistic individuals may be unwilling to take responsibility for their actions or accept criticism or feedback from others.

It is worth noting that while these traits and behaviors are commonly associated with narcissism, they can vary in intensity and may not be present in all individuals with narcissistic traits. It is also important to recognize that individuals with narcissistic traits may be capable of change with appropriate treatment and support.

CHAPTER 2

THE GREAT CONSEQUENCES

Effects on relationships

Narcissism can have a profound impact on relationships with family, friends, and romantic partners. The following are some ways in which narcissism can affect these relationships:

Family relationships

Narcissistic individuals may struggle to maintain healthy relationships with family members. They may be dismissive of the feelings and needs of others, and may be more concerned with their own desires and achievements. This can lead to conflict and resentment, and may strain family relationships over time.

Friendships

Narcissistic individuals may struggle to form and maintain friendships. They may view others as objects to fulfill their needs and desires, rather than as individuals with their own thoughts and feelings. This can lead to a lack of trust and intimacy in friendships, and may result in a pattern of shallow and short-lived relationships.

Romantic relationships

Narcissism can have a particularly significant impact on romantic relationships. Narcissistic individuals may be charming and charismatic at the beginning of a relationship, but over time, their self-centered behavior and lack of empathy can lead to conflict and relationship breakdown. They may struggle to maintain long-term relationships, as their need for admiration and attention may lead them to seek out new partners once the initial excitement of a relationship has worn off.

Communication

Narcissistic individuals may struggle to communicate effectively with others, particularly when it comes to expressing emotions or showing vulnerability. They may be more interested in talking about themselves than listening to others, which can make it difficult for others to feel heard or understood.

Control

Narcissistic individuals may try to exert control over their family members, friends, or romantic partners in order to maintain their sense of superiority and control. They may be prone to manipulation, coercion, or even emotional or physical abuse in order to get what they want from others.

Self-esteem

Narcissistic individuals may struggle with feelings of insecurity and low self-esteem, which can lead them to seek out validation and attention from others. This can put a strain on relationships, as the constant need for admiration and attention may be difficult for others to fulfill.

Overall, narcissism can have a significant impact on relationships with family, friends, and romantic partners. It is important for individuals with narcissistic traits to seek out professional help and support in order to address these behaviors and improve their relationships with others.

Performance and career success

Narcissism can have a significant impact on work performance and career success, both positive and negative. The following are some ways in which narcissism can affect these areas:

Positive impact

Narcissistic individuals may be more likely to take risks and pursue opportunities that can lead to career success. They may be confident in their abilities and willing to take on challenges, which can help them to achieve their goals.

Negative impact

Narcissistic individuals may struggle with teamwork and collaboration in the workplace. They may be more interested in promoting their own interests and achievements than working with others towards a common goal. This can lead to conflict and dysfunction in the workplace, which can ultimately impact work performance and career success.

Lack of self-awareness

Narcissistic individuals may struggle with self-awareness, which can impact their ability to identify and address areas for improvement in their work performance. They may be more likely to blame others or external factors for their shortcomings, rather than taking responsibility and seeking out constructive feedback.

Difficulty with authority

Narcissistic individuals may struggle with authority figures in the workplace, as they may view themselves as superior to others and resent being told what to do. This can lead to conflict and tension in the workplace, particularly if the individual is in a position of leadership.

Lack of empathy

Narcissistic individuals may struggle with empathy towards coworkers and employees. They may be dismissive of the feelings and needs of others, which can lead to a lack of trust and respect in the workplace.

Burnout

Narcissistic individuals may be prone to burnout, as they may push themselves too hard in pursuit of career success. They may be more likely to ignore their own needs for rest and relaxation, which can ultimately impact their work performance and overall health.

Negative impact on leadership

Narcissistic individuals may struggle with leadership roles, as they may be more focused on their own achievements and success than on the needs of their team or organization. This can lead to a lack of trust and respect from employees, which can ultimately impact the success of the organization.

While narcissism can lead to positive outcomes in terms of career success, it can also have significant negative impacts on work performance and relationships in the workplace. It is important for individuals with narcissistic traits to seek out professional help and support in order to address these behaviors and improve their work performance and career success.

Physical and mental health

Narcissism can have significant physical and mental health consequences for the individual and those around them. The following are some of the most common consequences of narcissism:

Relationship problems

Narcissistic individuals often struggle with maintaining healthy relationships due to their lack of empathy and self-centered behavior. This can lead to problems with friends, family, and romantic partners.

Anxiety and depression

Narcissistic individuals may struggle with anxiety and depression, particularly if they experience rejection or failure. They may also struggle with feelings of emptiness or inadequacy, which can lead to these mental health issues.

Substance abuse

Narcissistic individuals may be more likely to engage in substance abuse as a way to cope with their feelings of inadequacy or to enhance their sense of self-importance.

Risky behavior

Narcissistic individuals may engage in risky behavior, such as reckless driving or substance abuse, as a way to prove their invincibility or enhance their sense of excitement and thrill-seeking.

Eating disorders

Narcissistic individuals may be more prone to developing eating disorders, particularly those related to body image, such as anorexia or bulimia.

Cardiovascular disease

Research has shown that narcissistic traits are associated with an increased risk of cardiovascular disease, possibly due to the stress and anxiety associated with the condition.

Chronic pain

Narcissistic individuals may experience chronic pain due to their tendency to ignore or dismiss their own physical needs and symptoms.

Workplace issues

Narcissistic individuals may struggle with workplace issues, such as conflict with coworkers, difficulty receiving feedback, and challenges with teamwork and collaboration.

Legal issues

Narcissistic individuals may engage in illegal or unethical behavior in order to achieve their goals, which can lead to legal issues and criminal charges.

Suicidal behavior

In some cases, narcissistic individuals may engage in suicidal behavior, particularly if they experience significant rejection or failure.

Narcissism can have a wide range of physical and mental health consequences, both for the individual and those around them. It is important for individuals with narcissistic traits to seek out professional help and support in order to address these behaviors and prevent negative consequences from occurring.

Legal and financial potential

Narcissistic behavior can have significant legal and financial consequences for the individual and those around them. Some of the considerably expected consequences include:

Legal trouble

Narcissistic individuals may engage in illegal or unethical behavior in order to achieve their goals, such as lying, cheating, or stealing. This can lead to legal trouble and criminal charges, which can have serious long-term consequences for the individual.

Financial problems

Narcissistic individuals may overspend or engage in risky financial behavior in order to maintain their image of success or importance. This can lead to financial problems, such as debt, bankruptcy, or even financial ruin.

Divorce

Narcissistic individuals may struggle with maintaining healthy relationships, particularly in romantic partnerships. This can lead to divorce, which can have significant financial and emotional consequences for both parties.

Workplace issues

Narcissistic individuals may struggle with workplace issues, such as conflict with coworkers, difficulty receiving feedback, and challenges with teamwork and collaboration. This may lead to disciplinary action or loss of employment.

Lawsuits

Narcissistic individuals may engage in behavior that leads to lawsuits, such as defamation or breach of contract. This can lead to significant legal and financial implications.

Loss of reputation

Narcissistic individuals may engage in behavior that damages their reputation, such as lying, cheating, or engaging in unethical behavior. This can have long-term consequences for their personal and professional life.

Public humiliation

Narcissistic individuals may struggle with criticism or rejection, which can lead to public outbursts or other forms of humiliation. This can have significant social and emotional consequences for the individual.

Loss of support

Narcissistic individuals may struggle to maintain healthy relationships with friends and family, which can lead to a loss of social support and emotional stability.

Overall, narcissistic behavior can have serious legal and financial consequences for the individual and those around them. It is important to address these behaviors and prevent negative consequences from occurring.

Impact of social media

Social media has had a significant impact on our society, including how we perceive ourselves and others. It has also been linked to the exacerbation of narcissistic tendencies, particularly in younger generations. Here are some of the ways in which social media may contribute to the development or reinforcement of narcissistic traits:

Attention-seeking behavior

Social media platforms are designed to encourage users to seek attention and validation through likes, comments, and followers. This can lead to a focus on appearance and presentation, as well as a desire to portray a perfect life or image online.

Comparison culture

Social media allows users to easily compare themselves to others, which can lead to feelings of inferiority or a need to constantly one-up others. This can lead to a focus on self-promotion and self-enhancement, as well as a need for external validation.

Filter bubbles

Social media algorithms are designed to show users content that they are most likely to engage with, which can create filter bubbles that reinforce pre-existing beliefs and biases. This can lead to a reinforcement of grandiose or entitled beliefs.

Cyberbullying

Social media has also been linked to an increase in cyberbullying, which can both cause and exacerbate feelings of insecurity and inferiority.

Social media has the potential to both exacerbate and reinforce narcissistic tendencies in individuals. It is important to be aware of these potential effects and to use social media mindfully, in a way that promotes healthy self-esteem and positive relationships. This may include setting boundaries, limiting time spent on social media, and seeking support if needed.

CHAPTER 3

THE ROAD TO RECOVERY

Recognizing and acknowledging tendencies

Recognizing and acknowledging one's own narcissistic tendencies is crucial in addressing and overcoming narcissism. Some of the justifications why this is so important include:

Improved relationships

Narcissistic individuals often struggle with maintaining healthy relationships due to their lack of empathy and self-centered behavior. By recognizing and addressing their own narcissistic tendencies, individuals can improve their ability to empathize with others and form deeper, more meaningful relationships.

Better mental health

Narcissistic individuals may struggle with anxiety, depression, and other mental health issues due to their constant need for validation and attention. By acknowledging their own narcissism, individuals can begin to address these underlying issues and improve their mental health and well-being.

Increased self-awareness

Recognizing one's own narcissistic tendencies can help individuals develop greater self-awareness and insight into their own behavior and motivations. This can help them identify negative patterns and make positive changes in their life.

Improved self-esteem

Narcissistic individuals often struggle with low self-esteem and may rely on external validation to feel good about themselves. By acknowledging their own narcissism, individuals can begin to develop a healthier sense of self-esteem and self-worth.

Increased accountability

By recognizing their own narcissistic tendencies, individuals can take responsibility for their behavior and actions, rather than blaming others or external circumstances. This can lead to increased accountability and a greater sense of personal responsibility.

Improved decision-making

Narcissistic individuals may struggle with making sound decisions due to their tendency to prioritize their own needs and desires above all else. By acknowledging their own narcissism, individuals can begin to make more thoughtful, considerate decisions that take into account the needs and perspectives of others.

Overall, recognizing and acknowledging one's own narcissistic tendencies is an important step in overcoming narcissism and improving one's personal and professional relationships, mental health, and overall well-being.

Steps to change behavior patterns

Changing narcissistic behavior patterns can be a challenging process that requires dedication and effort. Some steps that can be taken to address narcissistic tendencies and promote healthier behavior patterns include:

Recognize the problem

The first step in changing narcissistic behavior patterns is to recognize the problem and acknowledge the need for change. This involves being honest with oneself about one's behavior and the impact it has on others.

Seek professional help

Narcissism can be a complex and difficult issue to address, and it may require the help of a mental health professional. A therapist or counselor can provide support, guidance, and strategies for overcoming narcissistic behavior patterns.

Develop empathy

Narcissistic individuals often struggle with empathy, as they tend to prioritize their own needs and desires above those of others. Developing empathy involves actively listening to others, putting oneself in their shoes, and considering their perspectives and feelings.

Practice self-reflection

Narcissistic individuals may struggle with self-reflection, as they tend to avoid looking at their own flaws and weaknesses. Practicing self-reflection involves being honest with oneself about one's behavior, motivations, and emotions, and identifying areas for improvement.

Develop healthy coping mechanisms

Narcissistic individuals may struggle with managing their emotions and coping with stress and anxiety. Developing healthy coping mechanisms, such as exercise, meditation, or journaling, can help individuals manage their emotions in a healthy and constructive way.

Practice gratitude

Narcissistic individuals may struggle with appreciating the contributions of others and recognizing the positive aspects of their life. Practicing gratitude involves focusing on the good things in life and expressing appreciation for the people and experiences that bring joy and fulfillment.

Set healthy boundaries

Narcissistic individuals may struggle with setting healthy boundaries and respecting the boundaries of others. Setting healthy boundaries involves communicating clearly with others about one's needs and expectations, and respecting the boundaries of others.

Practice humility

Narcissistic individuals may struggle with humility, as they tend to prioritize their own accomplishments and successes. Practicing humility involves recognizing the contributions of others and acknowledging one's own limitations and weaknesses.

Changing narcissistic behavior patterns requires a commitment to self-reflection, empathy, and personal growth. It is important for individuals to practice self-care and healthy coping mechanisms. With dedication and effort, it is possible to overcome narcissistic behavior patterns and develop healthier, more fulfilling relationships and a greater sense of self-awareness and personal growth.

Real-life individuals success

There are many real-life examples of individuals who have successfully overcome narcissism and developed healthier behavior patterns. Here are a few examples:

Tony Schwartz

Tony Schwartz is a well-known author and journalist who struggled with narcissistic tendencies for much of his life. He has written extensively about his experiences, and how he was able to overcome his narcissistic tendencies through therapy, self-reflection, and a commitment to personal growth.

Eric Schneiderman

Eric Schneiderman is a former New York State Attorney General who struggled with narcissistic tendencies throughout his career. He sought therapy and treatment for his narcissism, and has spoken openly about his experiences and the importance of seeking help for mental health issues.

Pete Walker

Pete Walker is a therapist and author who has written extensively about his experiences with narcissistic abuse and how he was able to overcome his own narcissistic tendencies through therapy and self-reflection.

Mariah Carey

Mariah Carey is a well-known singer and performer who has spoken openly about her struggles with narcissism and how she was able to overcome them through therapy and a commitment to personal growth.

Andrew Yang

Andrew Yang is a former presidential candidate who has spoken openly about his experiences with narcissism and how he was able to overcome his tendencies through therapy, meditation, and self-reflection.

These individuals serve as examples of how it is possible to overcome narcissism and develop healthier behavior patterns through self-reflection, therapy, and a commitment to personal growth. While the journey may be difficult, it is important to remember that change is possible, and that seeking help and support is a critical step towards achieving personal growth and emotional well-being.

Role of therapy and support recovery

Therapy and support groups can play a critical role in helping individuals recover from narcissism and develop healthier behavior patterns.

Therapy can provide a safe and supportive environment for individuals to explore their thoughts, feelings, and behaviors, and gain insight into the underlying causes of their narcissism.

A trained therapist can help individuals identify negative patterns of behavior, develop healthy coping mechanisms, and work towards building more positive relationships with others.

Cognitive-behavioral therapy (CBT) and dialectical behavior therapy (DBT) are two common types of therapy that can be particularly effective in treating narcissism.

CBT focuses on identifying and changing negative patterns of thought and behavior, while DBT teaches individuals how to regulate their emotions and build healthy interpersonal relationships.

Support groups can also be a valuable resource for individuals recovering from narcissism. Support groups provide a safe and supportive environment where individuals can share their experiences and learn from others who have gone through similar challenges.

Narcissistic Abuse Recovery groups, for example, can help individuals who have experienced emotional or psychological abuse at the hands of a narcissist to heal and move forward in their lives.

In addition to therapy and support groups, there are a variety of self-help resources available for individuals recovering from narcissism. Self-help books, online forums, and mindfulness practices can all be valuable tools for building self-awareness, cultivating empathy, and developing healthier behavior patterns.

It's important to remember that recovery from narcissism is a journey, and there may be setbacks along the way. But with the help of therapy, support groups, and self-help resources, individuals can develop the skills and insights necessary to overcome.

CHAPTER 4

STRATEGIES FOR MEN

Recognizing tendencies in men

Narcissism can manifest differently in men than it does in women, and there are some common narcissistic tendencies that are more frequently observed in men. Here are some examples of these tendencies, as well as tips for recognizing them:

Grandiosity

Men with narcissistic tendencies may have an exaggerated sense of their own importance, and may believe that they are entitled to special treatment or privileges. They may also have an inflated sense of their own abilities and accomplishments, and may be quick to take credit for the successes of others.

Lack of empathy

Men with narcissistic tendencies may struggle to understand or care about the feelings of others, and may be dismissive or contemptuous of those who they perceive as weaker or less important than themselves. They may also be unwilling or unable to take responsibility for the harm they cause to others.

Domination and control

Men with narcissistic tendencies may seek to dominate or control those around them, either through overt means like intimidation or coercion, or through more subtle means like emotional manipulation. They may also be highly competitive and unwilling to compromise or collaborate with others.

Aggression

Men with narcissistic tendencies may be prone to angry outbursts or even physical violence, particularly when their grandiosity is challenged or they feel that they are not receiving the attention or respect they believe they are entitled to.

Sexual entitlement

Men with narcissistic tendencies may view their sexual partners as objects to be used for their own pleasure, and may be dismissive or contemptuous of their partners' needs or desires. They may also engage in risky sexual behavior or use sex as a means of exerting power and control over others.

Recognizing these narcissistic tendencies in men can be challenging, as they may be highly skilled at hiding their true nature or projecting a charming and charismatic persona. However, some alert signs to look out for include:

- Exaggerated self-importance or a sense of entitlement
- A lack of empathy or concern for others
- An intense need for control or dominance in relationships
- Angry outbursts or aggressive behavior
- Tendency to accuse others for problems or failures

If you suspect that someone you know may have narcissistic tendencies, it's important to seek support and guidance from a therapist or other mental health professional. A professional can help you navigate the complex dynamics of a relationship with a narcissistic individual, and can provide strategies for setting boundaries and protecting yourself from emotional harm.

Specific strategies for men

Overcoming narcissism is a challenging process that requires commitment, self-awareness, and a willingness to change. Here are some specific strategies that men can use to overcome narcissistic tendencies and build healthy relationships:

Seek therapy

Narcissism is a deeply ingrained personality trait, and it can be difficult to overcome without professional help. A therapist can help you develop insight into your own narcissistic tendencies, and can provide guidance and support as you work to change your behavior patterns.

Practice empathy

Narcissistic individuals often struggle to understand or care about the feelings of others. Practicing empathy involves making a conscious effort to put yourself in other people's shoes, and to truly listen to their thoughts and feelings. This will help you build stronger and more meaningful relationships.

Cultivate humility

Narcissistic individuals often have an inflated sense of their own abilities and accomplishments. Cultivating humility involves acknowledging your own limitations and weaknesses, and recognizing that others have valuable insights and contributions to make.

Practice self-reflection

Narcissistic individuals often have a blind spot when it comes to their own behavior patterns. Practicing self-reflection involves taking an honest look at your own actions and motivations, and being willing to acknowledge areas where you need to improve.

Develop healthy coping mechanisms

Narcissistic individuals may use grandiosity, manipulation, or aggression as coping mechanisms when they feel threatened or vulnerable. Developing healthy coping mechanisms, such as mindfulness or meditation, can help you manage stress and anxiety in a more constructive way.

Practice gratitude

Narcissistic individuals often take their own accomplishments and privileges for granted. Practicing gratitude involves recognizing and appreciating the contributions of others, and acknowledging the ways in which you have been supported and helped along the way.

Take responsibility for your actions

Narcissistic individuals may be quick to blame others for their problems or failures. Taking responsibility for your own actions involves acknowledging your mistakes and making amends where necessary.

By incorporating these strategies into your life, you can start to overcome narcissistic tendencies and build stronger, more meaningful relationships with the people around you. It's important to remember that this is a process, and that change may not happen overnight. However, with time, commitment, and support, it is possible to overcome narcissism and lead a more fulfilling life.

Tips for navigating work and career

Recovering from narcissism is a process that can take time, and it can be challenging to navigate the workplace while working on personal growth and change. Here are some tips for navigating work and career as a recovering narcissist:

Set realistic goals

As you work on overcoming narcissistic tendencies, it's important to set realistic goals for yourself at work. Focus on achievable goals that are aligned with your strengths and interests, and take on new challenges gradually.

Practice active listening

Narcissistic individuals may struggle to truly listen to others and take their feedback into account. Practicing active listening involves making a conscious effort to hear and understand the perspectives of others, and to respond thoughtfully to their feedback.

Seek feedback and support

As you work on overcoming narcissism, it can be helpful to seek feedback and support from others in the workplace. Ask trusted colleagues or mentors for their input on your performance, and be open to constructive criticism.

Cultivate healthy relationships

Building healthy relationships with colleagues and superiors can help you navigate the workplace more effectively. Focus on building relationships based on mutual respect, trust, and collaboration.

Practice humility

Cultivating humility involves acknowledging your own limitations and weaknesses, and recognizing the contributions of others. Embracing humility can help you build stronger relationships and become a more effective team member.

Avoid attention-seeking behavior

Narcissistic individuals may engage in attention-seeking behaviors, such as taking credit for others' accomplishments or seeking out praise and recognition. As you work on overcoming narcissistic tendencies, it's important to avoid these behaviors and focus on contributing to the success of your team.

Stay accountable

Taking responsibility for your actions and being accountable for your mistakes is an important part of overcoming narcissism. If you make a mistake or cause harm to others in the workplace, be willing to take responsibility and make amends where necessary.

By incorporating these tips into your work and career, you can navigate the workplace more effectively and continue to work on personal growth and change. Remember that recovery from narcissism is a process, and that it may take time and effort to fully overcome these tendencies. However, with dedication, support, and self-awareness, it is possible to build a fulfilling and successful career while working on personal growth and change.

CHAPTER 5

STRATEGIES FOR WOMEN

Recognizing tendencies in women

Narcissistic tendencies can manifest in both men and women, but the expression of these tendencies may differ based on gender and cultural expectations. Here are some common narcissistic tendencies in women and how to recognize them:

Self-centeredness

Narcissistic women may be excessively focused on themselves and their own needs, often to the detriment of others. They may struggle to empathize with others and prioritize their own desires and interests above all else.

Need for attention

Like their male counterparts, narcissistic women may have an insatiable need for attention and validation.

They may seek out praise and recognition, and may become upset or defensive if they do not receive the level of attention they desire.

Exaggerated sense of self-importance

Narcissistic women may view themselves as uniquely talented, intelligent, or special in some way. They may overestimate their abilities and accomplishments, and may struggle to accept feedback or criticism.

Manipulative behavior

Narcissistic women may engage in manipulative behavior to achieve their goals. They may use their charm, flattery, or sex appeal to influence others, or may resort to more deceptive tactics like lying or gaslighting.

Difficulty with relationships

Narcissistic women may struggle to form and maintain healthy relationships. They may be prone to volatility and emotional outbursts, and may struggle to form intimate connections with others.

Disregard for others' feelings

Narcissistic women may lack empathy for others and may disregard their feelings or needs. They may be dismissive of others' concerns and may prioritize their own desires and interests above all else.

Recognizing these tendencies in oneself or in others can be a challenging process, but it is an important step in working towards change and growth. If you or someone you know is struggling with narcissistic tendencies, seeking professional support and guidance can be a valuable resource in the process of recovery.

Specific strategies for women to overcome

If you recognize narcissistic tendencies in yourself and want to overcome them, here are some specific strategies for women to help you build healthy relationships:

Seek therapy

Working with a therapist who is experienced in treating narcissistic tendencies can be an important step in the recovery process. A therapist can help you gain insight into your behavior patterns and help you develop new coping skills and strategies.

Practice self-reflection

Taking time to reflect on your behavior patterns, emotions, and relationships can help you gain insight into your narcissistic tendencies. Try to identify situations in which you have acted in a self-centered or manipulative way, and work to understand why you acted in that way.

Cultivate empathy

Building empathy can be a key component of overcoming narcissistic tendencies. Practice putting yourself in others' shoes and imagining their perspectives, and work to respond to others in a way that is considerate and compassionate.

Focus on relationships

Narcissistic tendencies can make it difficult to form and maintain healthy relationships, but making an effort to prioritize your relationships can help. Try to be present and engaged in your interactions with others, and work to understand their needs and feelings.

Develop humility

Humility is an important counterbalance to narcissistic tendencies. Try to develop a sense of humility by acknowledging your limitations and mistakes, and by recognizing the value and worth of others.

Practice self-care

Narcissistic tendencies can be fueled by insecurity and a need for external validation, so it's important to prioritize your own self-care. Take care of your physical and emotional needs, and try to cultivate a sense of self-worth that is not dependent on external validation.

Practice forgiveness

Forgiveness, both of yourself and others, can be an important step in the recovery process. Try to let go of grudges and resentments, and work to approach your relationships with a sense of openness and forgiveness.

Overcoming narcissistic tendencies is a challenging process, but with patience, commitment, and support, it is possible to build healthy relationships and live a fulfilling life. Remember to be gentle with yourself throughout the process, and don't hesitate to seek support if you need it.

Tips for balancing career and family

If you are a recovering narcissist who is trying to balance a career and family, there are some tips that can help you navigate this challenging balance:

Prioritize relationships

As a recovering narcissist, it can be easy to become overly focused on career success and external validation. However, it's important to remember that healthy relationships are the foundation of a fulfilling life. Make an effort to prioritize your relationships with your partner, children, and other loved ones.

Practice active listening

Narcissistic tendencies can make it difficult to truly listen to others, but active listening is an important skill for building healthy relationships. Make an effort to listen to your partner and children, and work to understand their perspectives and needs.

Set boundaries

As you work to balance your career and family responsibilities, it's important to set clear boundaries. This can include setting limits on work hours or commitments, and prioritizing time with your family.

Be present

Make an effort to be fully present in your interactions with your family, whether that's during meal times, outings, or other activities. Put away your phone and other distractions, and focus on engaging with your loved ones.

Practice self-care

As a recovering narcissist, it's important to prioritize your own self-care. This can include setting aside time for exercise, hobbies, or other activities that help you recharge and feel fulfilled.

Communicate openly

Open and honest communication is essential for healthy relationships. As you work to balance your career and family responsibilities, make an effort to communicate openly with your partner and children about your needs, expectations, and limitations.

Seek support

Balancing a career and family can be challenging for anyone, and it can be especially challenging for those who are recovering from narcissistic tendencies. Don't hesitate to seek support from a therapist, support group, or other resources that can help you navigate this balance.

By prioritizing relationships, practicing active listening, setting boundaries, and taking care of yourself, you can successfully balance your career and family responsibilities as a recovering narcissist. Remember to be patient with yourself throughout the process, and to seek support when you need it.

CHAPTER 6

STRATEGIES FOR KIDS AND TEENS

Signs in children and teenagers

Narcissistic tendencies can be seen in children and teenagers as well as in adults. Some signs of narcissistic tendencies in children and teenagers may include:

Lack of empathy

Children and teenagers who exhibit narcissistic tendencies may struggle to understand and respond to the emotions of others. They may appear insensitive or dismissive of other people's feelings.

Grandiose thinking

Children and teenagers who exhibit narcissistic tendencies may have an inflated sense of self-importance. They may believe that they are better than their peers and that they deserve special treatment or recognition.

Attention-seeking behavior

Children and teenagers who exhibit narcissistic tendencies may crave attention and validation from others. They may go to great lengths to be the center of attention, or to receive praise and admiration from others.

Entitlement

Children and teenagers who exhibit narcissistic tendencies may feel entitled to special treatment or privileges. They may become angry or resentful if they feel that they are not receiving the recognition or attention they believe they deserve.

Difficulty handling criticism

Children and teenagers who exhibit narcissistic tendencies may struggle to handle criticism or negative feedback. They may become defensive, dismissive, or hostile in response to feedback from others.

Lack of accountability

Children and teenagers who exhibit narcissistic tendencies may struggle to take responsibility for their actions. They may blame others for their mistakes, or avoid admitting fault or apologizing.

It's important to note that many children and teenagers exhibit some of these behaviors at times, and it does not necessarily mean they have narcissistic tendencies. However, if you notice these behaviors consistently and over a prolonged period of time, it may be worth seeking support from a mental health professional who can provide a comprehensive assessment and support for the child or teenager.

Tips for healthy self-esteem

Developing healthy self-esteem is an important part of a child's development, and it can help them build positive relationships, cope with stress, and achieve their goals. However, it's important to note that there is a difference between healthy self-esteem and narcissism. Here are some tips for helping children and teens develop healthy self-esteem without becoming narcissistic:

Encourage positive self-talk

Help your child develop a positive inner dialogue by encouraging them to talk positively to themselves. Encourage them to focus on their strengths and accomplishments, and to avoid negative self-talk or criticism.

Teach empathy and kindness

Encourage your child to think about the feelings and needs of others. Teach them to be kind and considerate, and to show empathy towards others.

Model healthy behavior

Children learn by watching the behavior of others, so it's important to model healthy behavior yourself. Avoid excessive focus on appearance, status, or material possessions, and instead model healthy relationships, self-care, and gratitude.

Praise effort, not just achievement

It's important to recognize and praise your child's achievements, but it's equally important to recognize and praise their effort and hard work. Help them see that success is not just about winning or achieving, but about the effort and determination that goes into achieving their goals.

Encourage healthy risk-taking

Encourage your child to take healthy risks and try new things. This can help them build confidence and self-esteem, while also developing important skills and abilities.

Avoid excessive praise

While it's important to recognize and praise your child's accomplishments, it's also important to avoid excessive praise or constant praise. This can create an environment where children become overly focused on achievement and external validation.

By promoting healthy self-esteem, empathy, and positive behavior, you can help your child develop a healthy sense of self-worth without becoming narcissistic. If you have concerns about your child's behavior or development, it may be helpful to seek support from a mental health professional who can provide individualized guidance and support.

Parent Strategic modeling and prevention

As a parent, you play a key role in shaping your child's behavior and attitudes. Here are some strategies to help you model healthy behavior and prevent narcissistic tendencies in your children:

Practice self-care

Prioritize your own self-care and well-being. Model healthy behaviors such as exercise, proper nutrition, and adequate rest. This can help your child understand the importance of self-care and encourage them to prioritize their own well-being.

Focus on character development

Help your child develop strong character traits such as kindness, empathy, and resilience. Encourage them to value these qualities over external accomplishments or material possessions.

Foster healthy relationships

Model healthy relationships with family members, friends, and colleagues. Show your child how to communicate effectively, resolve conflicts, and treat others with respect and kindness.

Encourage humility and gratitude

Help your child develop a sense of humility by acknowledging the contributions of others and showing appreciation for the help and support they receive. Encourage them to express gratitude for the people and things in their life.

Avoid over-praising or over-criticizing

Avoid excessive praise or criticism of your child's behavior. Instead, provide constructive feedback and encourage them to take responsibility for their actions. Focus on effort and progress, not just results.

Foster independence and responsibility

Help your child develop a sense of independence and responsibility by giving them age-appropriate tasks and chores. Encourage them to take responsibility for their actions and learn from their mistakes.

Encourage empathy and understanding

Teach your child to understand the feelings and perspectives of others. Encourage them to show empathy and compassion towards others, and to treat others with kindness and respect.

By modeling healthy behavior and values, you can help prevent narcissistic tendencies in your children. Every child is unique, remember, and will have different needs and challenges. If you have concerns about your child's behavior or development, it may be helpful to seek support from a mental health professional who can provide individualized guidance and support.

CONCLUSION

Overcoming narcissism is a challenging process, but it is possible with the right support and resources. If you recognize narcissistic tendencies in yourself, it is important to take the necessary steps to address them. Here are some reasons why:

Improved relationships, Better mental and physical health, Career success, Personal growth and fulfillment.

It is important to remember that overcoming narcissism is not a quick or easy process. It may require seeking support from a mental health professional, joining a support group, or making significant changes to your behavior and thought patterns.

The rewards of this journey however will be life-changing. By taking the necessary steps towards overcoming narcissism, you can create a more fulfilling and healthy life for yourself and those around you.

Yes, recovery from narcissism is absolutely possible and worth pursuing. While the journey can be challenging and require significant effort, the benefits of overcoming narcissistic tendencies are immense.

Recovery can lead to improved relationships, better mental and physical health, increased career success, and personal growth and fulfillment.

It is important to remember that recovery is a process, and it may not happen overnight. It may require seeking support from mental health professionals, joining a support group, or making significant changes to your behavior and thought patterns.

However, with patience and dedication, it is possible to develop healthier relationships, cultivate a more positive self-image, and live a more fulfilling life.

It can be helpful to remember that you are not alone in this journey. Many people have successfully overcome narcissistic tendencies and have gone on to live happy, healthy lives. By acknowledging your tendencies and committing to change, you are taking an important step towards a brighter future.